Sports Bag

words by Nigel Croser
photographs by Lisa James

Here is a sports bag. It is full of balls.

Balls are used in many sports. They are used in many ways.

This ball is for playing basketball. We can throw it, catch it, and bounce it. Some players can slam dunk it.

This ball is for playing tennis.
We can bounce it and throw it up.
We can hit it.

This ball is for playing soccer.
We can kick it, head it, or throw it.

Some players can catch it.

This ball is for playing softball.

We can throw it and hit it.

We can catch it with a glove.

This ball is for playing golf. We can hit it a long way or a short way. Sometimes we have to look for it.

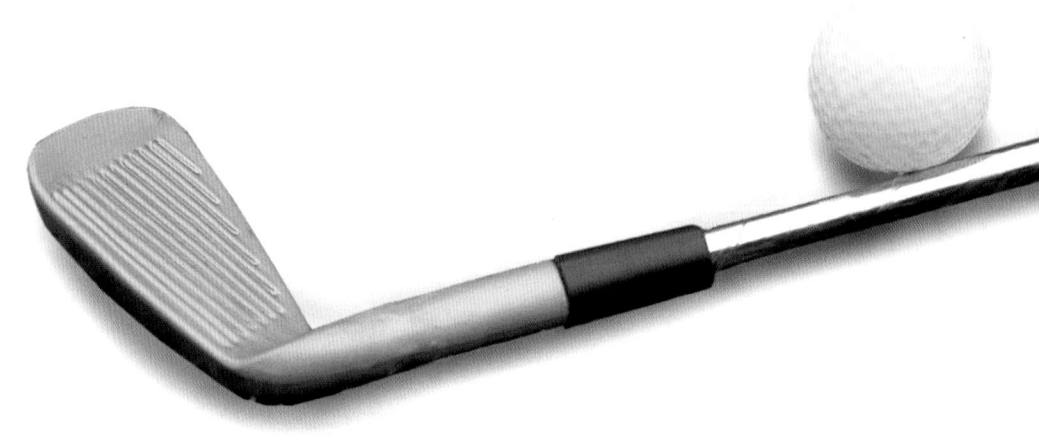

Here is a paper bag.

It is full of balls too.

These balls are for eating.

All sports players need good food.